Uncanny Clydeside

by M J Steel Collins

BeulAithris
Publishing

First published in 2017 by
Beul Aithris Publishing
Orkney Street Enterprise Centre
18 – 20 Orkney Street
Glasgow
G51 2BZ

www.beulaithrispublishing.co.uk

Dedicated to Sarah, the best Banshee impersonater in
Govan;
Michael, who I will one day beat at Pointless;
and the motely crew that is Team Spooky Isles.

Contents

Ghosts in the Railways

When it comes to heavy industry, shipbuilding is more synonymous with the Clydeside region. "Clyde built" was a by-word for quality when it came to the vast numbers of ships pouring out of the Clyde yards. Glasgow however, was no shirker when it came to the railways. The UK as a whole went into something of a railway frenzy in the early 19th century with the first railway in Glasgow being the Garnkirk to Glasgow line, opening in 1830. By 1900, there were four major stations serving a relatively small area: they were Queen Street, which opened in 1842; Buchanan Street in 1849, St Enoch's in 1876 and Central Station in 1879.

Glasgow took to train construction with almost the same enthusiasm as it did shipbuilding. Murdoch and Aitken of Hill Street Foundry constructed the first Scottish built locomotive in 1831 for the Monkland and Kirkintilloch Railway. From then until the 1840s, a variety of small scale manufacturers and two main workshops undertook train manufacture. Big changes started in the 1850s, when Glasgow and Southwestern Railway moved its workshop to Kilmarnock. At the same time in Springburn, Caledonian Railway made St Rollox their workshop, moving from Greenock, whilst North British Railways took over the Edinburgh and Glasgow workshop in Cowlairs. In 1903, Springburn exploded as a centre of train manufacture when several small locomotive companies merged to form the North British Locomotive Company, owning the Atlas and Hydepark workshops. North British was the largest locomotive manufacturer in Europe, producing over 28,000 engines between 1903 and the early 1960's, when steam engines gave way to the diesel variety.

The 1960's were not kind to the four stations in Glasgow City Centre. Dr Beeching's axe fell on St Enoch and Buchanan Street Stations in August and November 1966. The loss of St Enoch Station is still mourned today. A curious haunting involved the old St Enoch Hotel which was built around the train station. Ghosts were often encountered walking around the hotel cellar, made all the more interesting when you realise that St Enoch Square is in fact consecrated ground. It was the site of St Enoch's Chapel, which was demolished in 1925. Allegedly, St Thenew, mother of St Kentigern/ St Mungo of Glasgow was buried in its cemetery. It's thought that the ghosts seen in the hotel cellar were the spirits of those laid to rest in the cemetery. The train station and hotel themselves sat on the ground of the former surgeon's hall and underneath this consecrated land lies St Enoch's Subway Station, more of which will be covered later. The large, glass topped St Enoch Shopping Centre now sits where the old train station and hotel once were.

The small village of Grahamston was cleared to make way for Central Station. The urban myth goes that the streets of Grahamston still lie below Central's great edifice, but as romantic as it sounds, it's not quite true. The building which houses the Grant Arms pub and a building in Union Street are all that remain of the village. Central Station opened in 1879, however, it very quickly became congested, and in 1890, the Argyle Street bridge was expanded, with a ninth platform added to it. More serious measures were taken between 1901 and 1905, when the Station was extensively enlarged. Thirteen platforms were built, the original bridge raised by 30 inches and a new bridge built over the Clyde. Further modernisation occurred at the 20th century wore on.

The nature of ghost stories in the Central is somewhat abstract, but a few uncanny experiences have been reported. One example is given on a discussion on ghosts and hauntings on the Hidden Glasgow forums. Whilst on the low level platforms, a waiting passenger witnessed the strange sight of a man dressed in black and wearing a top hat walking along the railway tracks. A train arrived at the station, and left. But the man was still walking along the tracks. The low level of Central was originally separate to the station, as they were built for the Subway, which as we will discover, has several strange legends of its own. Another, better known tale, relates to one of the boiler rooms, which staff are reported to be too scared to enter alone lest they see the apparition of a woman with straggly hair. The legend is that she was murdered by her husband for her life insurance during the Great Depression. The couple hailed from Newton Mearns and had gone out for a walk early one evening, ending up at the station. The husband had lost everything in the Wall Street Crash and had secretly taken out a large life insurance policy in his wife's name. When the couple arrived at Central, he took his wife to one of the boiler rooms and murdered her. The tale states that the murderer was executed for his crime at Barlinnie Prison, yet, when The Ghost Club made enquiries about this following their August 2013 investigation of Central, nothing came up in the archives. Quite a few strange things happened during The Ghost Club's investigation, though in the report, they say that some were either accidental, or could be explained.

A strange experience was had in a room that had been used as a temporary mortuary. The team members there felt very uneasy. A major train crash occurred in 1915 during World War One, in which 227 died, including soldiers heading out for the Front. Central Station was the nearest major station and so bodies of the victims were brought here for processing. Other occurrences involve strange glimpses of apparitions, which appear from the report to be shadows of the past re-enacting life in the Central, from old staff to, soldiers and passengers.

Another Central ghost is mentioned by the late Peter Underwood in his 2013 book *Where The Ghosts Walk*. He describes the apparition of a businessman clutching a briefcase having been seen by passengers on trains. The story goes that it is the ghost of a businessman who was murdered for the £200 he carried in his briefcase. An experience involving the ghost of the businessman is described by Terence Whitaker in *Scotland's Ghosts and Apparitions*. As Whitaker notes, the experience is very similar to a ghost encounter in Newcastle, where a soldier lost in the fog is guided to the train station by a very friendly man. After boarding the train, the friendly man then goes on to tell the soldier about a nasty experience he had a few years earlier on another foggy night. The man was attacked and stabbed by a fellow passenger on his train, and died!

In the Glasgow version, during the First World, a junior doctor at the Western Infirmary gets lost in a fog trying to get to Central so he can go home to Motherwell. He bumps into a businessman who guides him to the station, and as they are both using the same train, share a compartment. The businessman tells the young doctor that he was taking this train a few years earlier, and found himself sharing a compartment with a suspicious looking workman, eyeing up the businessman's briefcase full of cash. Suddenly, the workman attacked the businessman, stabbing him in the heart and taking the briefcase. The doctor remarks that the knife must have missed a major artery for the man to have survived. Of course, the businessman remarks that he died and promptly vanishes. Patrick Noon was hung at Barlinnie for the murder of a businessman, whose body was found when the Carlisle train pulled into Motherwell, the first stop after Glasgow Central.

The Grand Central Hotel in Gordon Street forms part of the frontage of Central Station. It originally opened in 1883, but closed down in the early 2000s, a shadow of its former self. After a £20 million, year long make over, in which many of the hotel's original features were uncovered, it reopened in 2011 as a premier four star hotel and it has long reputed to have been haunted. The main story related to hauntings tells of the ghost of a maid walking through the building. She apparently threw herself from one of the upper floors after a love affair ended badly. A member of staff who worked in the hotel during the 1970s and 80s remembered doors opening and closing by themselves during the night. In 2012, a reviewer on Trip Advisor wrote about having a whale of a time during her two night stay. On checking in the hotel receptionist mentioned that it was haunted and she had a few interesting experiences. The first night proved to be an interesting one for our reviewer, who was woken up at around 1.30 am by a loud, inexplicable banging that carried on for 90 minutes, leaving her less sceptical on the subject of ghosts and haunting.

Some interesting stories can be found on the general railway. These range from the type that do the rounds with local children, such as the reminiscence on the Hidden Glasgow forums of the ten o'clock ghost train than ran through Priesthill, to the more tangible, yet inexplicable experiences of railway staff. During the 1970s, train guard James Tomlinson was doing the night shift when his train arrived at its service terminus Kirkhill Station in Cambuslang close to sunrise.

Walking across the bridge connecting the platforms as the train drew in, was a short middle aged man, wearing a trilby hat and carrying a briefcase. By time the train came to a stop, the man was standing on the platform apparently awaiting the return service.

Tomlinson turned to change the destination boards and when he looked back, the passenger had vanished. Tomlinson checked the train in case the passenger had boarded, but he hadn't, nor had he gone under the train. Anxiously, Tomlinson quickly alerted the driver and the booking clerk in the station, but neither had seen the passenger. Tomlinson was sure he had seen the man, but couldn't figure out what had happened, other than the fact that he may have just seen a ghost re-enacting a journey carried out several times in everyday life.

Another random spooky experience is described by Ron Halliday in his book *Haunted Glasgow;* in 1991, James Montgomery was waiting at Carntyne station, when he saw a young woman in her twenties approaching the platform. She was about five feet tall, with long brown hair and a duffel bag. The train arrived, and Montgomery went to urge her to hurry in order to catch it, but she wasn't there. It had seemed to Montgomery she was gliding, not walking and her feet weren't visible. Halliday says her description matches that of the victim of a suicide that occurred a few years earlier on the line into the station, but it's unclear whether the two are connected.

The Glasgow District Subway Company won its application to build a small, two tunnel underground railway in 1890. The tunnels, which are 6.5 miles in circumference took 6 years to complete. The Glasgow District Subway opened on 16 December 1896, and was immediately overwhelmed by an enthusiastic crowd, resulting in it having to be shut down for several weeks for more work. The system was privately operated, changing its name to Glasgow Subway Railway Company in 1922 (when the accident resulting in the Grey Lady at West St occurred). The daily operation of the system was carried out by the Glasgow Corporation Tramways, who eventually took ownership in 1923. The Corporation electrified the system in 1935, powering it from Pinkston Power Station. Prior to this, the underground was operated on a cable system, pulling the trains between stations. During the 1970s, the tired out system was overhauled, resulting in gaping holes around Glasgow. Some of the carriages running on the system at this point were new when the Underground opened. These of course were upgraded, the new stock being painted a fetching shade of orange, leading to the underground to be nicknamed The Clockwork Orange by Glaswegians, although the official name is the Subway, after being known as the Underground for several years. It is now operated by Strathclyde Passenger Transport.

A substantial ghost tour could be conducted around the Subway alone as during construction, the builders had to burrow through an old graveyard and even a plague pit. The pit was located between what became the Shields Road and West Street stations. The workmen noticed something was a bit odd when they started uncovering old teeth and bone fragments, plus the soil was unusual. It gave rise to the first ghost story associated with the Subway. The apparition of a small orb, no bigger than a golf ball would appear in the Shields Road/West Street section. The orb grew until it engulfed this the tunnel, and was called "The Clatter" due to the din it made, akin to the sound of several pots falling at once. Workers became nervous about having to work in this area. Those who were caught up in the apparition saw the tortured, twisted faces of the dead, believed to be plague victims unsettled by the work. The phenomenon stopped once the Subway opened.

Another entity associated with this part of the tunnel was The Ghoul, last sighted in 1955. Encountered several times by Subway staff, it appeared to have been something of a hybrid as its face was half human, half animal. In its last reported sighting, witnesses described the creature as eating raw meat, which they believed to have been stolen from a nearby butcher shop. The staff in this instance thought it was an insane boy, whereas others believed that it was a demon. A bona fide ghost linked to West Street station is that of Robert Cobble. Hailing from an affluent Glasgow family, he fell into poverty and took to drink, while also suffering from poor mental health. He would visit local pubs, telling tales of his associations with the Royal Family and his upbringing.

Cobble was a popular character, but one night, he was so severely assaulted during a robbery, he needed a walking stick and was visually impaired. This didn't stop him carrying on as usual, and he was said to have been quite a happy chap. He died after freezing to death outside West Street station in the early 1900s. His shivering apparition has since been seen huddled in the station entrance. Another ghost in that station is that of a Grey Lady, alleged to be the ghost of 30 year old Adelaide Carpenter or Simpson. The Glasgow Herald of 24 July 1924 reports that she was heading home from visiting her mother with her two-year-old daughter, when both fell on the tracks of the Inner Circle. Station Master, Robert McIntosh attempted to rescue them, injuring himself in the process. A train arrived seconds after the pair fell. Though the driver applied the brakes after seeing McIntosh signalling to him, the first carriage went over the top of mother and daughter. The toddler survived with surprisingly minor injuries – some bruising and broken fingers – but Mrs Carpenter was killed instantly. Her ghost is described as having a sad expression on her face and is either dressed in grey or has a grey complexion. Disembodied footsteps, sobs and whispers have been heard on the tracks, and maintenance staff reported seeing strange lights whilst repairing the track during the 1960s.

Moving over to the west of the city, Hillhead station has a couple of curious stories. One that seems to make its way more by word of mouth involves a woman who asks passengers if they have seen her son. There appears to be little else on the tale. Hillhead's other ghost is better known and reputedly friendly. It is the ghost of a well-to-do young woman in evening dress, who seems quite happy and has been seen several times over the years. She was seen in the 1970s by a maintenance worker repairing the tracks after the station had closed. The ghost was standing on the platform and as the station was shut, the worker made to go towards her, but she vanished. He and a colleague saw the apparition the following night. The sound of singing has been reported in the tunnels between Hillhead and Kelvinbridge stations.

Kelvinbridge itself is relatively quiet in terms of paranormal activity, though it has had its moments. One night, a cleaner heard voices cursing and swearing in the tunnel. Police investigated, but couldn't find anything. Workers in a building whose basement was situated next to the Subway reported hearing strange tapping during the night shift. Fearing a haunting, it was looked into, and it turned out to be the Subway maintenance worker tapping the tracks as he checked the state of the tunnels at night, when any required repairs are carried out. Still in the West End, a particularly gory apparition can be found near St George's Cross station. The figure of a man in Victorian clothes hanging in mid-air, head twisted to one side as though a rope was wrapped round his neck.

St Enoch's subway station has an interesting array of uncanny stories. During the Second World War, after a bombing raid, St Enoch's castellated booking office (now home to a café), had a bout of poltergeist activity. Green slime oozed from a wall, an office girl was knocked to the floor and an executive found his shoe laces inexplicably tied together. A ghostly cat has more recently been reported roaming St Enoch station by the night maintenance staff, though it appears to have been nothing more than an April Fool's joke, given that Strathclyde Passenger Transport put the report on the Subway website on 1 April 2013.

Ghost stories in the Govan car sheds at the long gone Greenhaugh Street pre-date the Subway's modernisation in the 1970s. Owing to the design of the car sheds, there was no direct access from the track, so carriages weren't brought in unless they needed repairs, when they would be lifted off the tracks by an overhead crane. They were stored in the tunnels when not in use. One night, a team was going down into the tunnels and passed the line of carriages enroute. They found a workmate standing by the last train talking to a middle aged man wearing a light coloured raincoat and a flat cap, who was believed to be a passenger who failed to disembark when the train went out of service at Copland Road (now Ibrox) station.

He was led by the maintenance team through the tunnels to the car shed, where he'd have been able to leave the tunnels and access the street. The team regularly looked back to check the passenger was still following, but were shocked to see he had vanished. They all agreed they had seen him, but couldn't explain his disappearance. The car sheds themselves were reportedly haunted by a strange figure that was seen in the driving cab of trains, but would vanish on being approached. The cabs were also extremely cold after the sightings.

A strange light was seen on the section of track that lay between where two maintenance teams worked one night. They couldn't explain it. Then in 1967, at 3AM one Sunday, pump man Willie Baxter had to walk through the tunnels between St Enoch and Bridge Street stations to fix a tank at Bridge Street. More than half-way through, he heard a strange noise like someone banging on the rails. The only person who could have made that noise was the ganger, who had already passed through the section not long before. Baxter was confused and scared at what was going on, and continued walking through the dark tunnels. He was near where the tunnel passed under the Clyde, where a ship's propeller turning in the river above could sometimes be heard, but Baxter discounted this. The noise got louder, and Baxter lost his nerve, haring back to St Enoch's. Later, talking about the experience with his workmates - it turned out that they also had similar experiences.

Clydeside Witchery

The Scottish Witch Hunts occurred at a time when society was in great flux; a lot was going on between the 16th and 18th centuries, which affected quite significantly not only Scotland, but the rest of the UK. As well as the witch hunt frenzy, there was the fall out of the Reformation, the English Civil War, the Covenanting Wars and the Jacobite Uprisings. Society was also becoming increasingly dominated by the growth of science and moving towards the Industrial Revolution. To say it was a time of great uncertainty is something of an understatement, however it does help to put things in historical and sociological context when looking at the Witch Hunts.

Prior to the arrival of Christianity in Scotland, belief in magic had existed for a number of centuries. It co-existed with the Church in what was perhaps an uneasy relationship. In an online article on King James VI and the Berwick Witch Trials, Caroline Emerick writes that the Catholic Church didn't punish suspected witches; instead they argued that it was silly for people to believe in witchcraft. The Church could still pursue suspected witches on the grounds of blasphemy, as very early cases show. Joyce Miller, in her book *Magic and Witchcraft in Scotland*, describes how there was a difference between actual witchcraft and everyday magic. Magic was used for good *(beneficium)*, such as healing, and accepted by the pre-Reformation church. During the Witch Hunt era, practitioners of *beneficium* were tried and sometimes executed as well as those practicing black magic, *maleficium*. The thinking behind the trials, as outlined by Hugh V McLaughlan, was that witchcraft was a wilful act. Whether it was used for good or bad, it was still a sinful act. People practicing it were in league with Satan and in opposition to God and society, making their condemnation justified.

The actual persecution for the act of witchcraft itself didn't occur until after the Reformation, which saw a radical change in thinking, and the introduction of the 1563 Witchcraft Act, making made witchcraft a capital crime for the first time. For the first few decades after the Act was passed, there were limited trials and executions, but they were scarce. It took off in the first of several witch hunting frenzies following the Berwick Witch Trial of 1590 that saw James VII of Scotland become seriously involved in eradicating witchcraft. This came about when witches allegedly prevented James' betrothed, Anne of Denmark from reaching Scotland after causing storms that made her ships turn back to safety. James himself set out to fetch her, and his own ship was earmarked by witches both in Denmark and Scotland to go down in a squall on his way back to Scotland - except they targeted the wrong ship.

At the time, there was a frenzy regarding practicing witches in Denmark. It's believed that James VII spoke to Niels Hemmingson, a Danish Lutheran from whom the King may have received the idea of the Satanic Pact. This is the suggestion that witches renounce their baptism in order to serve Satan; it became influential in Scotland and could be seen in charges laid against witches during the latter era of the Witch Hunts. James VII wrote a book on witchcraft, *Daemonologie,* in 1597. Following the Berwick Witch Trials, a local commission could be granted by the Privy Council, the highest legal power in Scotland, for witches to be tried in local courts, although this was removed in 1597 after James VII grew uneasy at the large number of trials. In several cases, it was a case of warring families or neighbours taking things to the extreme, accusing each other of witchcraft, or threatening to curse; a fairly risky thing to do at the time. Later on however, it was possible for local authorities to apply to the Privy Council for Commissions to try suspected witches, which eased the pressure on an overburdened High Court in Edinburgh.

Trying a witch was quite a complex affair. At first, suspected cases were investigated by the Kirk sessions, comprising of the minister and church elders. The Presbytery and Synod looked into more complex cases. Cases ranged from the positive use of magic in healing and charming, to the malign. Torture for witches was sanctioned in Scotland, mainly consisting of sleep deprivation. It was rare for witches to be ducked. Once the Kirk was satisfied by a witch's guilt, they were passed over to the State to be dealt with. Trials were either held in Edinburgh, or in circuit courts headed up by travelling judges. McLaughlan writes that nowadays, the trials and investigations are viewed as irrational and unjust, with the innocent being found guilty after being induced to confess by torture and subsequently being executed. He points out that a lot of investigation went into the cases, and that not all witches were executed, indeed some were acquitted. Still, the figures are incredibly high. It's estimated that about 2,000 were killed, but it was probably considerably higher and women figured highly in these. Those sentenced to death were strangled before being burned at the stake.

There were peaks and troughs in the eagerness to track down witches. The first big wave came after the Berwick Trials, a second from 1620, by which time James VII had ascended the English throne, becoming James I south of the border, and ruling from London. Two more waves erupted in the 1640s. Whilst Cromwell ruled the UK, there were fewer trials, as the English judges running the Scottish legal system were sceptical of witchcraft. Another peak occurred after the Restoration of the Crown, but with the approach of the 18th century and the influence of The Enlightenment, witch trials occurred less frequently. The Church was keener than the State to pursue them, the latter being less convinced by the existence of witchcraft. In 1735, the Witchcraft Act changed, and it was no longer a capital crime. It's thought the last witch burning in Scotland occurred in 1724. It was during this later era that perhaps two of the most notable cases within the vicinity of Glasgow and Renfrewshire occurred, made more unusual by the growth of rational thinking causing more doubt about the plausibility of witchcraft.

In 1676, a major case occurred on the Pollok estate, involving Sir George Maxwell of Auldhouse, who owned the estate. The Maxwell family lived in Pollok Castle, across the White Cart River from the village of Pollok-town. Sir George was a staunch Covenanter and a businessman, who had previous involvement with other witch trials, including the aforementioned Inverkip case. A contemporary account of the Pollok Witches case, written by Sir George Maxwell's son[1], John, begins:

"Upon the 14th of October, 1676, my father was surprised at Glasgow, in the night time, with a hot and fiery distemper; and coming home the next day, he was fixed to his bed. The

---

[1]   Found in *"A History of the Witches of Renfrewshire who were burned on the Gallowgreen of Paisley"* 1809, facsimile appearing in *The Kirk, Satan and Salem: A History of the Renfrewshire Witches* ed Hugh V McLaughlan . Sir John Maxwell had included an account of the case in a 1684 letter to George Sinclair, Professor of Philosophy at Glasgow University.

physician, fearing a pleurisy and a fever, opened a vein, and the application of medicaments being made, the fiery heat was abated, --he remaining for seven weeks together under a great pain, chiefly in his right side, though not fixed to his bed. There had come to Pollok-town a young dumb girl, but from whence was not known, who had remained there for four weeks before, but seldom frequenting Sir George Maxwell's house, til at length she came to some more familiarity and converse with his two daughters. And, having observed Sir George sick and weak in his body, she signified unto them –That there was a woman, whose son had broke into his fruit-yard, that did prick him in the sides."

The 'young dumb girl' was one Janet Douglas, a 13 year old vagrant, who has come to be regarded by some to be a charlatan. The woman whom she pointed out was a local by the name of Janet Mathie. Mathie's son, Hugh Stewart, had recently been partaking in a bit of scrumping in the Castle fruit garden with one of the Maxwell servants, who later confessed to Sir George. It was after this that Mathie was alleged to have created an effigy of Sir George, sticking pins into it to cause him ill health. At first, Maxwell's daughters were reluctant to believe Douglas, however two of his servants thought it worth investigating, and accompanied the girl to Janet Mathie's house. Once there, Douglas pulled out an effigy, stuck with a pin in each side. Mathie was duly arrested for witchcraft and taken to prison in Paisley.

Under questioning, Mathie denied the accusations, saying that Douglas had fabricated the whole thing. The Sherriff-Depute ordered Mathie to be searched for witch marks using a witch pricker, who allegedly found several. Meanwhile, the pins had been removed from the effigy of Sir George

19

Maxwell, and he made some recovery, though not to any notable degree according to his sons. Janet Mathie remained in jail, and the rumour mill went into overdrive over what evil deeds she could have carried out. Sir George fell ill again in January 1677, and was so sick his family feared for his life. As Sir John Maxwell later wrote, *"But they were more surprised on the 7th of January, being the Sabbath Day, when they had an express from the dumb girl, who was at Pollok-town, but could not get over the water to the house, the river being so swelled at the time, signifying that John Stewart, Mathie's eldest son, had four days since formed an effigy of clay, for taking away Sir George's life."*

The effigy was found hidden in the straw of John Stewart's bed, and both he and his 14 year old sister Annabil Stewart were arrested. Annabil succumbed first to intense questioning, followed by her brother after witch marks were 'found' on him. Their confessions were in the hyperbolic fashion of other witchcraft confessions of the era. Annabil described the manufacture of the effigies and cursing of Sir George Maxwell. Another three women were named in the confessions – Marjory Craig, Bessie Weir and Margaret Jackson, Janet Mathie's 80 year old mother in law. Mathie, it was claimed, had dedicated her son and daughter to Satan's service whilst they were still in the womb. When they were old enough to agree to this, Satan visited, and both John and Annabil renounced their Baptism and gave themselves to the Devil. Annabil described how they had been given witches' marks by Satan nipping, and later, that she had 'lain' with him.

The others implicated were arrested. Margaret Jackson soon caved into questioning and confessed. Marjory Craig and Bessie Weir denied the charges. It was claimed that Janet Mathie had a series of run-ins with the Maxwell family, and the effigies were made as a form of retribution. John Stewart had made the second effigy in an angry response to his mother being imprisoned. All six were charged with witchcraft and the first day of the trial was held in Paisley on 27 December 1677. Annabil and John Stewart repeated their fantastic confessions. That night, Janet Mathie was ordered to be placed in stocks, thought to be an attempt to prevent her committing suicide. The stocks were particularly heavy and difficult to move; Mathie was shackled a few feet away from her bed. In the morning, the warders found her, still in stocks, asleep in bed. The trial was further fuelled by Janet Douglas just over a week before the trial, who led to the discovery of an effigy of one of Maxwell's daughters in Mathie's cell.

The trial reconvened at Paisley on 15 February. This saw Mathie, Weir and Marjory Craig, all continuing to deny being witches, face the three who confessed in court. Annabil and John Stewart pleaded with their mother to confess. All six were convicted. Owing to her age, Annabil Stewart was spared the death penalty, but her brother, Janet Mathie, Margaret Jackson, Marjory Craig and Bessie Weir were strangled and burned on Gallowsgreen in Paisley on 20 February 1677. Sir George Maxwell died in April that year. Janet Douglas had in the meantime become capable of speech and hearing. She continued a short career journeying round as a witch finder, before winding up in Edinburgh, where she was arrested and charged with several offences which led to her being whipped and transported. In a letter to George Sinclair, Professor of Philosophy at Glasgow University, Sir George Maxwell's son, John, described meeting Janet Douglas. She tells him she has no memory of her parents, only that she was called Janet Douglas and that she had been treated badly as a child. As to how she became 'dumb', Douglas said she suffered a 'swelling' of the tongue and throat, losing her speech, but recovered it by applying *Album Groecom*, a paste of honey and desiccated dog faeces. As to how she could tell whether someone was a witch:

"She answered, that she had it only by a vision, and knew all things as well as if she had been personally present with them; but had no revelation or information from the voice of any spirit; nor had she any communication with the devil or any spirit of that kind; 'only,' says she 'the devil was represented to me, when he was in company with any of the witches, in that same shape and habit as he was seen by them'"

A curious footnote to the case is that Janet Douglas could apparently understand Greek and Latin, though hadn't received previous tuition in the languages.

The following appeared in the Paisley Presbytery records of December 30, 1696:

"This day Mr Turner represented to the Presbytery a deplorable case of Christian Shaw, daughter of the laird of Bargarran, in the paroch of Erskine, who since the beginning of September last, hath been under a very sore and unnatural-like distemper, frequently seized with strange fits, sometimes blind, sometimes deaf and dumb, the several parts of her body sometimes violently extended, and other times a violently contracted, and ordinarily as much tormented in various parts of her body, which is attended with an unaccountable palpitation in those parts that are pained, and that those several weeks by past she hath degorged a considerable quantity of hair, folded up straw, unclean hay, wild-fowl feathers, with divers kinds of bones of fowles and others,

together with a number of coal cinders, burning hot candle grease, gravel stones ,etcetera, all which she puts forth during the forementioned fits, and in the intervals of them is in perfect health wherein she gives an account of several persons, both men and women, that appeares to her in her fits, tormenting her..." (89)

It refers to the strange case of Christian Shaw and the Bargarran Witches, which seems like a seventeenth century amalgamation of the plots from *The Exorcist* and *The Exorcism of Emily Rose*. Christian was the 11 year old daughter of the Laird of Bargarran House, near Erskine. Her apparent bewitching started shortly after a series of seemingly small events in August 1696. The Shaw's maid, Katherine Campbell was caught stealing milk by Christian. Both fell out after Christian told her mother of the theft, with Katherine cursing Christian to the effect of hoping that the Devil would hurl her soul through hell. A few days after, Agnes Naismith, a local widow, appeared at Bargarran, asking Christian after her health. Naismith had a less than enviable reputation as a venomous and evil minded woman, already thought to be a witch. A few days after, Christian began suffering a series of bizarre fits, symptoms of which included: trance-like states, extreme bodily contortions, feats of immense strength, seeming to be deaf, blind and lacking the power of speech and vomiting strange objects such as needles, hot coal, animal faeces, bones and warm candle wax.

At first, Christian was taken to see doctors in Glasgow, who were left bewildered. At a loss for any other explanation, they came to the conclusion that the girl was a victim of witchcraft. Christian claimed to be the victim of numerous unseen attackers, including the Devil. She named several people as her tormentors, including Katherine Campbell and Agnes Naismith. Naismith visited Christian and prayed for her, after which, Christian said the old woman no longer attacked her. Campbell refused to have anything to do with Christian and continued to be accused of tormenting her, resulting in the maid being arrested and put in custody. Others named by Christian included a tenant farmer on Bargarran, John Lindsay of Barloch and a Highlander visiting the house. Christian reacted so badly to them, that her father imprisoned both on the spot.

Her behaviour became increasingly strange; Christian claimed her invisible assailants would scratch, throttle and threaten her, trying to force her to become a witch, which she refused to do. The girl's strange fits also continued. As well as the trance-like states, contortions and vomiting of strange objects, Christian would also float and levitate, as described in the later pamphlet on the case:

"She was suddenly carried away...through the chamber and hall, and sixteen large steps of a winding stair up toward the top of the house...but was carried down...toward the gate again, where accordingly, she was found, and was carried up as formerly, all the parts of her body distended and stiff as one dead [2]*"*

A commission was established by the Privy Council to investigate the case, and more named individuals were arrested, including Alexander Anderson, a beggar, and his daughter Elizabeth. She soon told her inquisitors that whilst she herself wasn't a witch, her father was. She had witnessed several

---

[2]   Quoted in *Poltergeist Over Scotland* by Geoff Holder, The History Press 2012, p 41

meetings her father took part in, and had also seen the Devil. Elizabeth gave the names of those she saw at the meetings, where plans were made to harm several people, including Christian Shaw. Some of the names given by Elizabeth matched those already provided by Christian, whilst others were new. The authorities arrested those accused, including brothers Thomas and James Lindsay, Margaret Lang and her daughter Martha Semple, James Reid and Margaret Roger. Elizabeth had also named others already in custody, including John Lindsay of Barloch and the mysterious Highlander. Agnes Naismith had presumably long been in custody by this point. Lang, Semple and Roger were taken to see Christian, who confirmed they were among her assailants. The young Lindsay brothers, aged only 14 and 11, confessed all, naming those already identified by Christian and Elizabeth Anderson. Charges being lined up included murder as well as witchcraft, as according to Elizabeth Anderson and the brothers, stated the accused had also killed, in some cases using the power of spells. Two babies had died locally under mysterious circumstances; a ferry sank, drowning two people and a minister had died of a fever after the witches had burned his likeness in a fire.

Twenty-four were named in the application from the Commission to the Privy Council to go to trial, though by time the trial started in March 1697, a further three had been charged. Facing trial were Agnes Naismith, the young James and Thomas Lindsay, Katharine Campbell, Alexander Anderson, Jean Fulton, Margaret Fulton, James Reid, two older Lindsay brothers, John and James, Margaret Lang, Margaret MacKillope, Margaret Ewing, William Miller, Margaret and

Janet Roger, John Lindsay of Barloch and several others [3]. Owing to the amount of evidence, the trial concluded in May 1697, by which time several people had been released for a variety of reasons. Margaret and Janet Roger had confessed and were released for showing repentance, the younger Lindsay brothers were released due to their young age which made them unfit for trial and Elizabeth Anderson was released after giving evidence in court. Three people died whilst in prison: Alexander Anderson, Janet Fulton and James Reid. Anderson's cause of death appears lost in the mists of time, whilst Janet Fulton had died of old age and James Reid committed suicide by hanging himself with his hanky.

As for Christian, her afflictions came to an end in March, and she was bothered no more. In the end, seven of the accused were sentenced to death by strangulation and burning, which took place on 10 June 1697. At Gallowsgreen in Paisley, Katherine Campbell, Agnes Naismith, brothers John and James Lindsay, John Lindsay of Barloch, Margaret Lang and Margaret Fulton were executed. Their ashes were placed in an urn and buried at the crossroads at Maxwellton Cross in Paisley under a horse shoe as a reminder of what happened. The horse shoe mark is still there, though recently replaced. It's unclear if the urn is still there, as it would have been disturbed over the years with the various roadworks.

[3]   Julian Goodare, Lauren Martin, Joyce Miller and Louise Yeoman, 'The Survey of Scottish Witchcraft', http://www.shca.ed.ac.uk/witches/ (archived January 2003, accessed '[29/09/15]').

The case of the Bargarran Witches was the last mass witch execution in Scotland. Shortly after, two pamphlets detailing the events were published, both with highly descriptive and long titles. One was published in London by a 'T.P', entitled: *A RELATION OF THE DIABOLICAL PRACTICES Of above Twenty WIZARDS and WITCHES Of the Sheriffdom of Renfrew in the Kingdom of Scotland, CONTAIN'D In their Tryalls, Examinations, and Confeffions, And for which feveral of them have been Executed this Prefent Year, 1697.* This has been reproduced at times to accompany re-enactments of the trial in Paisley. The other, seen by experts as having 'borrowed' heavily from the slightly earlier pamphlet detailing the Salem Witch Trials, which took place in Massachusetts, America, in 1692 and 1693. This is entitled: *A True Narrative of the Sufferings and Reliefe of a Young Girle; Strangely molested by Evil spirits and their instruments in the West: With a preface and postscript containing Reflections on what is most Material or Curious either in the history or trial of the Seven Witches who were Condemn'd to be Execute in the country,* believed to be written by John MacGilchrist, Christian Shaw's uncle, and the Reverends James Brisbane and Andrew Turner. The latter was reprinted twice in the 19th century in books sharing the title *The Witches of Renfrewshire,* which also featured the Pollok Witches.

The case still continues to be controversial. Down the years, Christian Shaw came to be regarded as a fake, an attention seeker who sent innocent people to their death. Nowadays, it's believed she may have suffered a childhood ailment that she later grew out of. She had no recurrence of her symptoms as an adult, and in fact went on to be a successful business woman, running a textile business. The only other notable event was that she was widowed only two years after marriage. Her family were comfortable landowners and Christian had been taught to read and write. Much has been done on her case by academic Hugh V McLaughlin who edited *The Kirk, Satan and Salem: A History of the Witches of Renfrewshire* in 2006, featuring reprints of the 19th century books mentioned above.

A piece of Paisley folklore relates that Agnes Naismith, as she was about to be executed, uttered a curse on Paisley, which some people believe holds to this day, and in fact have attributed subsequent events in the town. One of these is the Paisley Canal disaster of 1811, in which 84 drowned when a barge capsized; the other is the heavy economic down turn faced by the town since the 1960s and from which, it is still recovering.

A Clyde Built Haunt in America

The Queen Mary is one of the most famous ships to have been built in the Clyde shipyards. At one point, the Clydeside was supplying the majority of the world's shipping, ranging from battleships and tankers to spectacular ocean liners such as the Queen Mary. They met a variety of fates, some good, some not so good. The Queen Mary got lucky. Whilst her sister ship, the Queen Elizabeth, met an ignominious ending after burning to a wreck in Hong Kong Harbour in 1972, The Queen Mary has enjoyed life as a tourist attraction and hotel in Long Beach, California for several years. She is also renowned as one of America's most haunted locations, apparently boasting something in the region of 600 ghosts, featuring heavily in paranormal TV shows, websites and books.

Planning for the Queen Mary began during the 1920s, when Cunard found itself having to contend with an aging fleet and stiff competition from other shipping companies. Working with the John Brown shipyard of Clydebank, Cunard planned to replace its three transatlantic liners with two state of the art super ships. Models of various designs were tested in a specially built tank at John Brown's to discover which best coped with the tough conditions at sea. On 28 May 1930, John Brown was awarded the contract to build the ship, code named 534, being the 534th construction at the yard. Before work could begin, there was a problem with insurance. Commercial insurers at the time could insure to a maximum of £2.7 million for an entire project, however 534 required coverage of £4 million for the hull alone. The British Government, which came to bear a strong influence on the fortunes of 534, stepped in with the Cunard (Insurance) Act December 1930, making the Government insurers for the ship's construction. The hull plate and keel had been laid by the end of January 1931.

As 534 was to be one of the biggest ships the world had ever seen, adjustments had to be made at various ports to accommodate her on the transatlantic route. Larger docking facilities were built in New York and Cherbourg, whilst in the UK, Cunard planned a dedicated port in Southampton, as the company's home port in Liverpool was too small. Enter the British Government again when the owners of the land designated for the ship were loathe to build facilities for just one ship. They were soon convinced, as the Government had already invested a lot of money into 534's construction. Industry across the UK also benefitted from the project, as parts were ordered from across the country to build the massive ship.

But the effects of the economic decline after the Wall Street Crash caught up with the enterprise, when on 10 December 1931, Cunard held an emergency board meeting to discuss how the company was faring in the Depression. It wasn't good. Profits had plummeted with a drop in passengers, and it was decided that it wasn't a good time to build a luxury ocean liner. Work on 534 halted the next day at the John Brown yard, with thousands of workers losing their jobs. It was a disaster all round. Socially and economically, Clydebank struggled, as families had no money to spend in shops and other local businesses, which in turn closed down. Children were turning up at school hungry and poorly clothed and the population's health declined due to lack of food. There was a national impact also, as the companies supplying parts for 534 were forced to lay off employees.

David Kirkwood, Member of Parliament for Clydebank, started a campaign to get work restarted on 534, believing it would rejuvenate the economy. The Government was reluctant, however, thinking it would be in bad taste to fund the construction of the Liner when there was hardly any money to finance the country. It was made even more bitter by the fact that, despite the Depression, the French Government was paying for the construction of the ocean liner, Normandie. Cunard also got in on the campaign, as their existing Transatlantic fleet was deteriorating and repairs were costly. Passengers were attracted by the more modern, faster ships of their competitors, and Cunard needed 534 completed in order to keep up. At one point, the Prince of Wales, later abdicating monarch Edward VIII, showed an interest in the campaign after meeting David Kirkwood at a party. As the campaign continued, 534 quietly rested in the scaffold at John Brown's, becoming home to a large number of rooks and earning the moniker The World's Largest Bird's Nest'.

Another reason for the Government's reluctance to fund building at this time was because of the difficulties faced by the other major British shipping company, The White Star Line, which was also subsidised by the government. Chancellor Neville Chamberlain felt that two subsidised shipping lines would be weak, but that joining the two would make them stronger. Additionally, the government could rely on shipping being available during war. Negotiations were held on the merger, the government pressing the issue of completing 534; if the government was to fund the rest of the project, then Cunard would have to accept joining with the White Star Line. In the end, the government agreed not only to fund 534, but also the construction of a sister ship, the future Queen Elizabeth.

Clydebank was jubilant. Workers were recalled to John Brown's on 3 April 1934, accompanied by nothing less than a pipe band. It also meant orders were restarted for requisite parts, for which the relevant companies had to take on new employees to meet demand. David Kirkwood, MP, was proven right in the effect the restart had on the British economy. Regular reports had to be provided to the Sovereign on the progress of 534's construction. There was the issue of what to name the new ship. Both Cunard and White Star had their own naming traditions for their ships; the former using names ending in –ia, and the latter using –ic endings. It was felt a break was needed.

The accepted tale is that on one of the regular updates to King George V, the King was asked if the ship could be named 'after one of the most illustrious and remarkable women who has ever been Queen of England', meaning Queen Victoria. However, the King took it another way, saying that it was the biggest compliment he and his wife, Queen Mary, had ever received and he would ask her when she got home. As it turns out, this is mere myth. The King and Queen were due to launch the ship anyway, so it was decided it would be sensible to name it after Queen Mary. There was also already a popular steamer plying trade round the Clyde estuary called Queen Mary, and the liner couldn't share the name. The steamer was renamed Queen Mary 2 to avoid confusion and a loss in lucrative tourist trade.

On 26 September 1934, the 534 was launched as the Queen Mary, with her regal namesake smashing a bottle of Australian Chardonnay off the bow (the usual custom of French wine was disposed of thanks to sore feelings over the Normandie). The newly named ship was taken to the fitting out basin for the additions of engines, boilers and the luxury accoutrements that make for a world class ocean liner. It was a massive job, taking well over a year, and several prestigious artists were brought in to design elite lounges and provide sculptures and other art. The Queen Mary left Clydebank on 24 March 1936, to a warm send off. At an overall length of 310.7 metres, height of 55.17metres and width of 35.97 metres, she was a tad large for the narrow River Clyde. At one point, the Queen Mary became stuck, earning an entry in the Lloyd's Register of Shipwrecks. Following her sea trials, during which she reached a speed of 32.84 knots (32.79 miles per hour/60.81 kilometres per hour), the Queen Mary was taken to her dock at Southampton and formally handed over to Cunard White Star.

She made her maiden voyage on 27 May 1936, reaching New York in four days, five hours and 40 minutes. Such was demand for her first trip, that the three class system was abandoned to make space for all the passengers. Much excitement was generated by the event, generating a lot of memorabilia and partying on both sides (and length) of the Atlantic. It was the start of a prestigious career, during which the Queen Mary became a firm favourite with celebrities and dignitaries alike. Shortly after her maiden voyage, the Queen Mary won the Blue Riband for speediest Transatlantic crossing from her rival, the Normandie.

Whilst the excitement surrounding the Queen Mary continued in her early years, the threat of war loomed large. The liner's crew had secretly been trained in what to do should conflict break out; on her last voyage to America immediately before war was declared, the Queen Mary carried a record number of Americans heading home from Europe to avoid the inevitable stramash, including comedian Bob Hope. On reaching New York, she was moored alongside her rival Normandie, and later her sister ship, the recently completed Queen Elizabeth. In March 1940, the Queens were called into war service, and after receiving a new, grey paint job, sailed to Australia for refitting as troop ships. The Queen Mary was nicknamed the Grey Ghost – fitting given her later haunted reputation.

All the sumptuous fittings were removed and the liners capacity was increased to carry large numbers of soldiers to where they were required at the various theatres of war around the world. The Queen Mary also carried prisoners of war, who were kept in rather unpleasant conditions at the depths of the massive vessel. Several are thought to have died and were buried at sea. Prime Minister Winston Churchill used the Queen Mary in order to travel to America for conferences with President Franklin D Roosevelt; this involved the setting up of Churchill's state rooms and accommodation for his large staff. There was a large bounty put on the Queen Mary, who saw her as a threat. Any U-Boat captain who managed to sink her was promised a lot of money, prestige and promotion. Consequently, the British Admiralty set a 'no stop' rule for the ship, in which she was not to halt for anything, in case it was a trap. In order to avoid the U-Boats, she had to maintain a zig-zag pattern whilst at sea, as it made it difficult for her to be tracked.

After the Americans entered the war in 1941, they were granted use of the Queens as troop transportation. The Queen Mary had her capacity increased once again, to carry tens of thousands of GIs. The liner was packed as a result. Troops took it in turn alternating between sleeping outside on deck and indoors. On return journeys, the Queen Mary was turned into a hospital ship, taking injured GIs home to America. It was on an outbound trip from America, when she was carrying 15,000 GIs that the Queen Mary was involved in a major disaster. On 2 October 1942, she met her escort just off the coast of

Donegal, Ireland, which was to see her safely through more treacherous waters at the end of her journey.

The escort consisted of six destroyers and one anti-aircraft cruiser. Whilst the Queen Mary followed her usual zig-zag route, the cruiser, the Curacao went off course, and into the path of the liner. The Curacao was sliced in half when the Queen Mary ran into her. In the ensuing chaos, 338 men drowned and 99 survived. The Queen Mary couldn't carry out a rescue mission, as the Admiralty's no stoppage rule was still in force. The remaining destroyers of the escort picked up survivors. After the war, a court case was held, in which the Queen Mary was apportioned one third of the blame and the Curacao two thirds. Compensation was paid by Cunard to the families of those drowned as the Admiralty were not responsible for this.

After the war ended in 1945, the Queens Mary and Elizabeth were still in service to the forces. First transporting troops home to America, followed by several voyages taking GI brides and their children from Britain to their new homes in the States. In September 1946, the Queen Mary was returned to Cunard, and went to her home port in Southampton for a refit. Staff were brought in from John Brown's for the job, which included repainting in Cunard colours and a replacement stern to remedy the damage caused by the Curacao incident. Both Queens took up liner duties, the Queen Elizabeth entering such service for the first time.

In the post-war period, the Queen Mary remained popular, holding the Blue Riband once more, until she lost it to the more modern liner SS United States in 1955. During the 1960s however, passenger numbers fell dramatically as air travel took off. The Queen Mary was also aging and in 1966, Cunard announced she was to be retired and put up for sale. In

1967, the City of Longbeach, California, bought the liner, and she sailed into town at the end of her last voyage in December 1967, escorted by a welcoming committee of several yachts. The Queen Mary saw further refurbishment, turning her from a ship into an 'official building', comprising of a hotel and a tourist attraction. The massive propellers were removed, as were the engines and boilers; and the new facility was open for business in 1972.

Stories of ghosts on the Queen Mary apparently surfaced not long after her arrival at Long Beach. Though, as Robert James and Anne Powell Wlodarski write in their book, *The Haunted Queen Mary*, there was great reluctance to make the haunting public knowledge owing to the way in which such things were viewed at the time. Maintenance and security staff regularly reported strange encounters in the depths of the ship, but mainly kept them amongst themselves. That's not to say the odd encounter didn't involve a member of the public; one woman was exploring Shaft Alley, the vast space where the engines once were, when she encountered what appeared to be an engineer looking doleful. Thinking it strange, she mentioned it to the security guard on leaving Shaft Alley. The guard went to check, but found no one there. The guard then asked the woman to come to the security office where she was shown photos of former crew; from this she identified one as the man she saw, a man known to be dead!

As time went on, attitudes began to change from fear of the paranormal, to curiosity towards it, and the ghosts of the Queen Mary became public knowledge. Today the ghosts are a staple of paranormal media, featuring in several books and TV shows. There are also official paranormal events regularly held on the ship, including a ghost tour and paranormal investigations. It's believed that about 600 ghosts haunt the Queen Mary, making it one of the most haunted locations in the US. Like a theatre, a structure such as the Queen Mary was so bustling and busy during working life at sea, she really couldn't be anything but haunted. Visitors, hotel guests and staff have caught fleeting glimpses of ethereal crew carrying out the tasks required in the functioning of a large ocean liner, and there have been a few outbursts of poltergeist activity. One woman working in an office on the Queen Mary thought she saw her boss entering her section, but when she looked, no one was there. In another experience, catering staff were setting up a breakfast buffet early one morning, when there came from the kitchen the loud sound of smashing crockery and other implements being thrown about. Rushing to the kitchen, they expected to find a huge mess. It was clear.

Another incident involving staff happened when several employees were taking their break in one of the ship's lounges. It suddenly seemed like there was a crowd of invisible people in the area. A sales assistant working late one evening in the Queen Mary convenience store was perplexed when a bag of potato chips began moving of its own accord. Guests staying in the hotel are no stranger to inexplicable happenings. Some have reported waking up feeling like they are sailing, impossible, given the ship is permanently moored in Long Beach; others have heard the banging of pipes, as if engineers are working on the ships. Guests have complained about their neighbours in the next room making loud noises at night, only to find that there is no room, only a corridor, immediately next to their cabin and then there are the reports of voices, appearing to be crew members in conversation. These hauntings seem to be of a residual nature, where events of the past are recorded in

37

the ether, and occasionally replay to those least expecting to encounter them.

Further activity reported in the guest cabins was featured in a two part special of British paranormal TV show, *Most Haunted*. In the First Class cabins, a male apparition, wearing 1930s clothing had been seen on several occasions. Guests also reported being woken by their bedclothes being pulled off them at night, hearing the sound of heavy breathing and seeing lights switch themselves on and off. On B deck, room B340 is no longer in use due to the amount of paranormal phenomena, including poltergeist activity, disembodied screams and eerie laughter reported. Guests placed here would frequently turn up at reception asking to be given a new room.

Eerie occurrences are regular experiences in the bowels of the ship, where the engines and boilers were located. Also in the lowest deck was once the Queen Mary's morgue, where bodies of crew and guests who died at sea were stored. This section was also where several prisoners of war were held in what would have been horrendous conditions. There was no air conditioning down here, causing much suffering. Some séances, including one that can be seen on *Most Haunted,* have apparently picked up the spirits of POWs who died on the ship. Other war related ghosts are claimed by some paranormalists to be victims of the Curacao incident. An entity identified as John Henry roams about the working decks of the liner. He appears to be the type who likes to be left in peace to do his own thing.

On the upper decks, where passengers enjoyed themselves during the Queen Mary's voyages, the past and the present seem to blend together at times. Occasionally, apparitional, well dressed passengers are glimpsed strolling around the main deck, or are heard. The sounds of people drinking have been heard in the liner's various lounges and cafes. In the main lounge, the vision of a woman, wearing a white evening gown, was frequently reported dancing to unheard music. According to the Wlodarskis, this particular entity appears to have an attachment to the piano that once stood in the Main Lounge. When the instrument was moved to Sir Winston's Restaurant and Lounge, the ghost was seen there. The heart of the Queen Mary's haunting is probably the First Class swimming pool; the public have restricted access, though can see it on tours and investigations. For the liner's ghosts, it's a 24/7 thoroughfare. The pool, now drained of water, is surrounded by two decks, has a diving board and adjacent changing rooms, where psychics have claimed there is a massive vortex, through which several spirits travel between the otherworldly realm and this one. There are a number of specific ghosts that have been seen, felt or heard in the pool. Perhaps the most poignant is that of Jackie, a young female spirit, whose voice has been caught talking to investigators on camera several times. She was identified by late psychic Peter James. The footage of Jackie talking can be viewed on YouTube. She was first recorded in the early 1990s, talking to James on American show, *Sightings*. In the early 2000s, she was recorded by investigators Bob Davis and Brian Clune.

There hasn't been anything, thus far, to explain who Jackie is. Two older female ghosts have been reported around the pool on several occasions by many people. One, dated to the 1930s, haunts the upper deck of the pool, whilst other, seemingly from the 1960s haunts the pool itself, swimming in what can only be ectoplasmic water. The apparition of an elderly lady dressed in a swimming costume and bathing cap has been seen a number of times, once confusing a tour guide who saw her about to dive into the empty pool. Strangely, this ghost is seen in black and white. Night time security were also bemused one night when the ghosts decided to have a party in the pool. The sounds of splashing, a ball being thrown about and laughing wafted from the pool; when security came to investigate - thinking it may have been some of the present day hotel guests having an impromptu, rather verboten, celebration – no one was there. Nobody living, at least.

A regular occurrence in the First Class pool is the appearance of wet footprints, outlining the bare feet of someone having just climbed out of the waterless pool. This was seemingly caught on camera by the *Most Haunted* team, who found the pool to be a hive of ghostly activity. One of the production team caught a fleeting glimpse of a woman sitting on the diving board, whilst the producer heard a piece of poolside tile skite by. American TV show *Ghost Adventures* also investigated the First Class Pool. Whilst they claimed to have found something demonic, other psychics and mediums have said that the ghosts of the Queen Mary are nothing but benevolent, even if they do give unsuspecting staff and guests a turn.

It seems rather apt for one of the most famous ships built on the Clyde to have found an afterlife as a renowned haunted hotel and tourist attraction out in California.

The Poltergeist's Knock

Poltergeists are a bewildering phenomenon. Countless cases have been documented going back to Ancient Rome and Greece where they have been variously described as demons, fairies, disembodied spirits, and the result of witchcraft and the unconscious mental powers of disturbed teens. The term itself derives from the German for "noisy ghost", *poltern* (noisy) and *geist* (ghost), first appearing in 1540 German dictionary, *Nuvum dictionarii genus.* It entered the English language in 1848 via Catherine Crowe's *The Nightside of Nature*, however there has been some argument that the term 'poltergeist' is outdated, as it is more than a 'noisy ghost'. The question is, what else could it be called? Poltergeist - as the term of a particular form of paranormal activity, and unbridled creepiness - has sunk into the public conscious and popular culture.

A wide range of activity is ascribed to poltergeists such as objects moving of their own accord, or flying violently through the air and being hot to the touch on landing. There is stone-throwing (lithobolia), where the homes of those infested by a poltergeist are pelted by rocks and stones, though it seems to be a feature of older cases; inexplicable knocks and rapping, which in some instances provides seemingly coherent responses to questions. Disembodied voices are a particular favourite of any self-respecting poltergeist. Items such as house keys, may go missing for weeks, only to be found in the most unlikely of places. Apparitions have also been reported in cases down the years, but are quite rare. Perhaps the most disturbing of all is the tendency of a poltergeist to physically attack people, slapping or hitting them with objects and causing them to levitate.

Currently, the hypothesis is that poltergeists result from the unconscious mental powers of a disturbed youth, brought about by the onset of puberty, sexual frustration and, well, adolescent minds in general. Poltergeists don't haunt a place, but people. The individual the phenomenon centres on is known as the focus. Several classic cases, such as the Columbia Poltergeist, The Sauchie Poltergeist and the Enfield Poltergeist have the focus as a preteen or teenage girl, frustrated and facing some upheaval in their lives. Adolescent boys also feature, for example, the Maryland case that inspired *The Exorcist*. But other cases have adults as their focus. And many, such as the Mackenzie Poltergeist, an ongoing case in Edinburgh, seem to feed off the energy of several people. So when it comes to poltergeists, there doesn't seem to be a hard and fast answer. The one common denominator seems to be that they come out of nowhere, terrifying and confusing the people at the centre of the commotion.

Towns and cities across the UK boast several poltergeist cases. The following, listing poltergeist cases in chronological order from the early 20th century shows the Greater Glasgow area is no different from the rest of Britain. A couple of early cases are to be found in the *Glasgow Herald*; on 23 October 1929, the newspaper carried a report of a tenement in Cowcaddens having to be guarded by the police from a crowd of curious onlookers. Mysterious rapping had been reported in a flat, and was subject to investigation by spiritualists. Another group of perhaps somewhat overeager spiritualists were turned away at the close door after appearing unannounced with the intention of carrying out a séance. The issue for 14 July 1958 carried the tale of American students studying at Glasgow University fleeing their tenement flat in Gibson Street because of a poltergeist. They had seen eggs and their breadboard dancing on their kitchen shelf and heard disembodied voices. One had approached the radio to turn it off, only for the device to switch itself off; meanwhile, the neighbours hadn't experienced anything unusual.

The *Glasgow Herald* casts doubt in its report on the poltergeist, instead arguing that the students weren't used to the everyday noises of Glasgow - the rumbling of the buses, neighbours coming and going and cats on the prowl. Interestingly however, the reporter did make note of an English friend living in a flat in Woodlands Road, not far from the students' flat, who regular held conversations with disembodied voice in his home.

In *Haunted Glasgow*, Ron Halliday details a haunting that took place during the 1960s and 70s at Paul Anderson's flat in Govan Cross, which produced poltergeist activity. One Friday evening at 5.30, Paul and his wife were talking in their living room; on the wall, a crucifix on a broken necklace hung from a nail, which also pinned a calendar to the wall. Suddenly, the crucifix began moving of its own accord, spinning and twisting on the nail and picking up speed. Paul and his wife clung to each other in terror, until the crucifix stilled. The cries of a baby were also heard in the flat, although there were no babies nearby. When he was moving out, Paul pulled the fireplace out in the bedroom, convinced he would find a baby's skeleton, but nothing was there.

Just across the Clyde from Govan lies Partick, the site of a few poltergeist cases in the 1960s and 1970s. One dating from 1968 was investigated by a reporter from the defunct Glasgow newspaper, The Evening Citizen. Shipyard worker, Lachlan Hanlon, and his wife Mary, had been scared to such an extent by a poltergeist in their Mansfield Street flat, that they had fled. It began with strange rapping which Lachlan joked about with Mary. However, the activity escalated; temperatures inexplicably dropped, a strange 'whirring noise' was heard and glowing shapes were seen floating over the couple's bed. A policeman had also seen Lachlan being thrown, screaming from his chair by an invisible force. As friends and workmates of the couple were cracking jokes about the haunting, the Hanlons agreed to return to the tenement with Evening Citizen Reporter Jim Brown to show the haunting was real.

To start the night, Lachlan sat close by the fire, reading aloud from parts of the Bible. He shivered and edged closer and closer to the warmth, to the extent that Jim Brown thought he must have been overheating, but Lachlan was cold to the touch. The poltergeist was more active whenever someone was in the bed recess, where two years earlier, a previous elderly tenant was found dying. Brown asked Mary to go into the recess, but she refused. The reporter then turned out the lights to see what would happen. A bizarre light appeared in the bed recess, just above the bed. The lights were switched back on when Mary started to scream. Afterwards, things were quiet until 2 AM, when the letter box began to rattle. After that they left the flat at the Hanlons' insistence. As yet, it's unclear what happened next. Today, Mansfield Street has been regenerated and forms part of the fashionable end of Partick.

A few years later, another young Partick couple found themselves the victims of a poltergeist. Kenneth and his partner awoke one morning to find their small tenement flat in chaos. The living room window had been broken, furniture was strewn everywhere, and every ornament, cup and plate in the flat had been reduced to piles of coloured sand. Intruders were ruled out as the front door of the flat was still locked. Somehow the living room window had been shattered from the inside. The couple slept in the living room's bed recess, and

44

hadn't woken during the night. Kenneth took his father's dog to the flat to investigate. The dog point blank refused to enter, and the couple moved out.

In the *Gazetteer of Scottish Ghosts*, Peter Underwood notes an undated Glasgow poltergeist case. A young family had just moved into a council flat with their six month old infant, when odd occurences began to take place that included raps, bangs and furniture moving of its own accord. The frazzled out family moved out. Investigators looked into the case and weren't disappointed. They encountered the usual panoply of poltergeist activity of crashes, bangs, and things moving by themselves. A medium was brought in and communicated with an entity that claimed to be the cause of the haunting. The ghost was a relative of the family, and was trying to get their attention to warn them about something stuck in the baby's throat. The family quickly arranged for an X-ray to be carried out; the infant had an operation the same day to remove an obstruction to the windpipe that could have caused suffocation.

James Montgomery experienced poltergeist activity most of his adult life. The case was first documented by Ron Halliday in *Haunted Glasgow*. James' first encounter was as young adult in 1971. His kitchen taps turned on and off by themselves, and a strange tar covered the ceiling of his flat. In 1992, James moved into a flat in Dennistoun, which was the scene of some very peculiar activity. The bedroom was colder than the rest of the flat, and was prone to filling up with smoke from time to time. There was also the sound of dishes being washed in the kitchen, when no one was actually in there. New wallpaper quickly lost its colour and strange apparitions were seen around the flat.

One of James' friends was using the bathroom and encountered a figure wearing shroud like clothing. A photo of James standing in one of the flat's doors showed a strange figure standing next to him. But strangest of all was the night he came home to find a shadow sitting in his favourite chair in the living room, unnerving him so much, he sat up all night. Poltergeist activity occurred in a new flat James had moved to by the early 2000s. Lights switched on and off of their own accord and an unknown voice called James' name. He and his home help also saw a shadow in the hallway. James left a tape recorder running to see what could be picked up, and recorded a series of swear words. He opted not to try that again.

A substantial poltergeist case, similar to the more famous Enfield Poltergeist of London in terms of scale, occurred in Balornock, North Glasgow between 1974 and 1975, predating its London counterpart by a few years. It involved two families living in the Northgate Quadrant; the Grieves and the Keenans. The Grieves family consisted of David, his wife Elizabeth, their sons Derek, aged 14, Jeffrey, aged 11 and Elizabeth's elderly mother; in the flat below them were the Keenans, consisting of James Keenan, his wife and their son Gordon, aged 30. Neither family saw eye to eye. Poltergeist activity started at 10 pm on 3 November 1974, when Derek and Jeffrey Grieves were awoken by loud knocking in their room. The noise followed them to their parent's room, where they went to get some sleep, continuing until 6 am. Believing that the Keenans had made the noise, the Grieves phoned the police, who had a word with the Keenans. However, the noise continued, disrupting the Grieves' sleep, resulting in the arrest of the Keenans.

While the Keenans were at Springburn police station, the rapping continued. David Grieve believed that somehow, one of the Keenans had given the police the slip and come home to continue playing their prank. When the Keenan's came home, a fight broke out, resulting in David Grieve getting convicted of assault. It soon became clear that the Keenans weren't at the source of the rapping. Charges against them were dropped and the conclusion was reached that perhaps something out of the ordinary was happening, however the Keenans made a formal complaint against how the police handled the case. Things escalated: the rapping continued, ornaments floated about and the cause of it all started knocking out the rhythm of "The Dead March", a piece of classical music by Handel. Elizabeth Grieve worked out a code for the entity to communicate using knocks and letters of the alphabet, the reliability of which has been seen as a tad dubious. Through Mrs Grieve's code, the entity stated that it was the spirits of miners killed in an accident down a mine where James Keenan was a manager. He was blamed for the accident. There was no evidence that Mr Keenan had actually worked in the mines. Nonetheless, Mrs Grieve received messages from these 'spirits', ordering Mr Keenan to be strangled. Life became even more bizarre for the Grieves. They fled to the home of Mrs Grieve's sister to escape the poltergeist, but it followed. The terrified families were treated to the sight of an ornament floating through the air, spinning a mirror on its swivel base, a music box playing itself, water dripping and a self-propelled trolley.

The police were still involved in the case, growing increasingly frustrated and turning in reports with classics such as "The bed moved in a northerly direction". Housing officials also became involved. They and the police visited the Grieves' and Keenans' homes at the same time. Both groups could hear knocking concurrently. The group in the Keenans swore that it came from the Grieves' flat; whilst those in the Grieves' said that the noise was coming from the Keenans' home. Things were getting complicated. The police asked the Rev. Murdo Ewan MacDonald, Professor of Practical Theology at Strathclyde University for assistance.

When Rev. MacDonald visited the Grieves', he encountered doors moving by themselves and alarm clocks going off. The day after, Rev. MacDonald received a call from Mr Grieve telling him that a coffee table had just levitated, whilst an ashtray flew across the room. With the assistance of Strathclyde University Chaplain, Rev. David Magee, Rev. MacDonald carried out an exorcism, which settled the haunting for a few weeks. In January 1975 however, it kicked off again. The Grieves had seen a news item about a poltergeist in Newcastle, and decided to record their experiences. A new school term had just started, much to the chagrin of Derek, who hated school. It's thought this may have played a part in reigniting the poltergeist.

The activity became more extreme, the rapping turning into loud bangs, which shook the flat. Again, the Grieves fled to relatives, where the chaos continued. When the Grieves returned home, they found their flat in chaos; furniture was thrown about and toys either smashed or stuffed down the toilet. Activity followed Derek to school, where pencils danced and doors slammed. When he was in his father's car, the electrics failed – as did the fuses in a relative's house when Derek came to visit. In January 1975, the case was reported in the *Glasgow Herald.* The poltergeist also targeted Jeffrey, who was a small boy, yet somehow he managed to kick a huge wardrobe away from a wall and overpower his uncle, who stood at six feet two inches and weighed 16 stones. Professor Archie Roy, the

Glasgow 'ghost buster', became involved in the case in February 1975.

Eventually, both boys became ostracised at school and the family's health began to suffer from the strain. A medium visited and claimed to have cleared the spirits, but the poltergeist remained strong. One of the boys attacked both Mr Grieve and Rev. MacDonald with impressive strength, whilst the poltergeist contorted the lads into strange positions. One day, Derek suddenly displayed impressive card tricks, which his parents claimed was possession by the aforementioned ghostly miners. A consultant psychiatrist from Dundee visited, and found no evidence of health problems or fakery.

On 23 May 1975, James Keenan passed away after a long illness. The poltergeist suddenly calmed down around this time, to which Mrs Grieve attributed to Mr Keenan's death; although it may also have had something to do with Derek Grieve being on holiday at his grandparents' in the Highlands. There was a brief resurgence of the case in late 1975, when Derek, having reached 15, had left school and was seeking employment, but it settled for good when he became an apprentice electrician.

Another poltergeist, and the final case of this chapter, occurred in Paisley in 1977. Known as the Glenburn Poltergeist, this targeted 13 year old Alan A., who lived with his mother. His father had walked out, and the family were also coming to terms with the death of Alan's grandfather, which affected him badly. Following the old man's death, Alan moved into his grandfather's bedroom. Alan was a big fan of Adam and the Ants, covering the room in posters of the band. One night, he couldn't sleep, and was sitting up reading a magazine. At 11.30 pm Alan heard a strange scratching, but couldn't find an explanation for it. He decided to ignore it, though it happened on successive nights, always between 11.30pm and 2 am.

One night, the noise got more extreme. From the attic came the sound of marching, though nothing was up there. Terrified, Alan called in his mother, who couldn't explain it. The various noises continued, until one night it got so bad that Alan and his mother fled. They went to the local priest for help, but were turned away. With no one to turn to, they chose to ignore it, hoping it would go away. Things got worse for Alan the night he saw a well-defined shadow on his posters. After that, he slept in the living room. Alan had a close group of friends, who noticed something was wrong. He told them about the haunting and they wanted to see it for themselves. After obtaining permission from his mum, the group of teenagers sat in Alan's room one night waiting to see what would happen. At 11.30pm, it began. One of the boys was so terrified, he tried to leave, but the door handle came off in his hands. Eventually, the haunting passed, leaving Alan with a fascination for the supernatural.

Ghosts, Galvanisation and Grave Robbers in the Ivory Towers

The University of Glasgow is the fourth oldest university in the English speaking part of the world and was established with the granting of a Papal Bull by Pope Nicholas in 1451. Early classes were held in the crypt of Glasgow Cathedral and the Chapter House of the Black Friars Convent in the High Street. The University was housed in various old buildings around the High Street and in former ecclesiastical buildings, until new premises, specifically constructed for the University were built on the same land in the early 1600s. These were described as "one of the finest specimens of Scottish architecture in the 17th century".

By the 19th century however, the buildings were in poor condition. In 1846, plans were mooted for the Glasgow, Monklands and Airdrie Canal to build a new campus at Woodlands and take over the High Street land, but nothing came to fruition. The City of Glasgow Union Railway Company bought the High Street College Lands in 1863, though the University stayed put until the new campus at Gilmorehill was ready in 1870. The new building, designed by Sir Gilbert Scott and his son in the Gothic Revivalist style, wasn't actually completed until the 1880s. It was massive in comparison to the old College Lands accommodation, which would have fitted comfortably in one of the quadrangles of the Gilbert Scott edifice. The University has expanded its campus considerably around the Gilbert Scott.

The old buildings at the High Street were demolished in the 1870s to make way for a railway goods yard and some parts of the old buildings made their way to Gilmorehill. Part of the original ornate stone gateway was carefully dismantled brick by brick and put into storage. In 1907, it was rebuilt as a gatehouse and lodge at the north east entrance to the University. This was funded by Govan MP and Fairfield Shipyard owner Sir William Pearce and the building was named the Pearce Lodge after him. It housed the Department of Naval Architecture until 1907, then the Student Representative Council until 1969. From then, it was utilised as an administration office. On the west wing of the Gilbert Scott building, leading to the University Chapel, the Lion and Unicorn staircase was re-erected. Both these are significant locations in Glasgow University's ghost stories.

There are two main tales on Gilmorehill. One relates a mysterious Grey Lady who has been seen in several places including Pearce Lodge, the Gilbert Scott Building quadrangles, Undercroft and Lion and Unicorn staircase. The Grey Lady's story goes back decades. One of the strange aspects about the Grey Lady is the varying descriptions given by those who have seen her. Logical deduction would have it that more than one ghost is doing the rounds, however, this is quite hard to ascertain. Descriptions range from the apparition appearing as a woman in a grey Victorian coat, with a cape round her shoulders, a girl in grey clothing dating from the 1920s to 1940s to a girl wearing a grey trench coat and plimsolls. As to her origins, they are vague, although there has been speculation that she may be the ghost of a female student who died in the early 20th century – that however, doesn't account for the apparition in Victorian garb, or indeed the little old lady in grey encountered by the porter in 1989. Such is the nature of ghost sightings.

The Grey Lady has been sighted by several members of University staff over the years, people, as one source put it "from all walks of life". One former student described being told on a freshers tour that the ghost haunted the quadrangles. The most active time for the ghost seems to be between 11pm and 5 am, when she has kept security on their toes. The middle of the night isn't when you would expect to see students on campus, not even ones pulling all-night study sessions. One guard described how the Grey Lady had been seen in the same place by several of his colleagues. Of her manifestations, he said that she just suddenly appears as guards walk around the quadrangles then vanishes, but can actually be seen standing there. One guard even checked underneath exam tables stored in the Undercroft, thinking the ghost was someone up to mischief and hiding underneath –of course no one was there.

As for the Pearce Lodge, the Grey Lady has been sighted there on a number of occasions. Norman Adams writes in his *Haunted Scotland* of the experience of a university porter in the Pearce Lodge in 1989. The porter saw an elderly lady clad in grey approach the door, and anticipated her ringing the doorbell. She didn't press the bell and was gone when the porter went to investigate. His workmates later told him he had seen the resident ghost, while other sightings include her appearing as just a face. Then there was the time the Grey Lady fully materialised in front of an unsuspecting secretary. The Pearce Lodge does however, have an additional haunting exclusive of the Grey Lady. In this instance, activity is focussed on the Lodge alone.

It's thought that whatever lurks in the Pearce Lodge followed from the old campus in the High Street. The story associated with it is that at some point there was a murder during that era of the University's history, resulting in a ghost. The aforementioned guard, who bore witness to the Grey Lady, also saw something in the turret window of the Pearce Lodge, having already heard strange stories associated with the building. On two occasions, always on a clear, moonlit night, he saw a figure standing in the second floor turret window. He wasn't sure if it was male or female. A colleague was also shaken to see the same figure. As the guard put it, late at night, with no one around, the campus takes on quite a different atmosphere.

There is a tale about a student who asked to be locked up in the Pearce Lodge all night as part of a bet. It wasn't a successful wager. Books started flying off shelves, and the terrified student had to be let out. There is also rumour of a room within Pearce Lodge that is permanently cold and can never be heated, which is kept locked up. Another group of brave students also lost their nerve one Rag Week when they asked to be let into the room. Staff had to let them out after the students reported hearing footsteps when no one else was there.

There are a few more, shorter tales, from Gilmorehill. The first relates to a bizarre photo that appeared in a university magazine. It was a shot of the Quadrangles, in which a figure wearing a stove pipe hat appeared, a figure who wasn't there when the picture was being taken. Another is tied to one of the older buildings on campus, a window overlooking the old Children's Hospital in Yorkhill that is eerily chilly. It is the haunt of the ghost of a young doctor, who apparently studied at the University Medical School and who stands looking at the hospital where they worked. On a related note, the Western Infirmary Lecture Theatre is also supposed to have a ghost, but the story is unclear. The Boyd Orr building, one of the University's 1960s additions, has tales of lifts that have minds of their own. Late at night, when the building is closed, the lifts still travel up and down, like they do during the working day, transporting people to various lectures, tutorials and laboratories. On inspection, the lifts were found to be empty.

Teaching Medicine at Glasgow University started in the 18th century. And in its earlier days, the medical school didn't escape the blight of bodysnatching. Admittedly, the University seemed to have copped some of the flack for the resurrectionist tendencies of the private medical schools around the cities. Anatomy, the subject area most associated with bodysnatching, was a subject treated with much suspicion. The University was attacked by local mobs on three occasions for teaching it, however it was a necessary evil. The Napoleonic Wars (1799 – 1815) cut off access to mainland Europe, preventing medical students from going over to study at continental schools, yet the Wars caused a huge demand for surgeons in the army. Both factors caused a huge surge in numbers seeking training in Medicine. There were a few hundred medical students in Glasgow in the 1820s.

In order to qualify as a surgeon, students studied Anatomy and had to dissect a body. This was something of an issue as bodies were in short supply. The only legally obtainable bodies were those of executed murderers, a provision of the 1752 Murder Act. This also allowed for murderers to be gibbeted after hanging, but this wasn't a popular practice in the west coast of Scotland. In all, only 32 people were executed for murder in the region during the time the Murder Act was in force. Not all of them made it to Glasgow for dissection, and some were even sent to the Edinburgh University Medical School. It was a case of too many students, not enough corpses.

This is where the bodysnatching helped to fill a gap. Students often went to cemeteries to get their own cadavers, aided in some cases by sextons and gravediggers, who found it to be a nice little earner on top of their meagre wages. A little later, it became somewhat more organised, with groups carrying out the grisly task of prising corpses from graves to sell to the Anatomists and their students. Some corpses didn't even make it to their own funerals, being spirited away by anyone from enterprising undertakers to poverty stricken relatives. Fresher cadavers commanded a higher price.

The most notorious bodysnatching case in Glasgow had no direct involvement with the University, though it did lead to prohibitions on bodysnatching on pains of expulsion being read out to students at the start of every session. On 13 December 1813, police officers witnessed suspicious characters fleeing from the Ramshorn Kirkyard. The next day, investigations revealed that the tomb of the recently deceased Mrs Janet McAllister had been violated and her corpse no longer there. An angry mob gathered outside the home of the University Anatomy Professor, Dr James Jeffray and smashed his windows, but he was innocent. The figures seen by police had ran in the direction of College St, where Dr Granville Sharp Pattison taught at a private medical school. Pattison had gathered a close coterie of medical students around him, all of whom had taken a kind of fraternity style oath not to reveal each other's secrets. They were encouraged to go bodysnatching by Pattison, who apparently believed it to be central to gaining an understanding of Anatomy.

So, it was with some reluctance the police were admitted, accompanied by Mrs McAllister's brothers and her dentist. A jaw bone and teeth found in a murky jar of water were identified as hers. Another search turned up several other severed body parts under the floorboards. Pattison, surgery teacher Andrew Russel and two students Robert Munro and John Maclean were charged with stealing Mrs McAllister's corpse. They were further accused of taking it to Pattison and Russel's rooms and 'mangling the body in a horrid and shocking manner, to prevent its being recognised by the relations' as the police were hammering the door. All four pleaded not guilty. The case seemed to hang on the identification of the jaw and teeth as Mrs McAllister's. Her dentist, Mr Alexander, produced teeth he said that he had made for Mrs McAllister and fitted to her mouth. The defence counsel had applied for the case to be held in private as it involved the revelation 'special circumstances of a very delicate nature'. This was denied.

In his address to the jury, the judge intimated that there was no doubt that the jaw belonged to Mrs McAllister, but left it up to them to determine whether this was enough to convince them that Pattison and co. were involved in lifting the body. Their defence had already cast aspersions on this, using medical expertise to rule out the other body parts discovered depending on time of death. The jury returned a verdict of Not Proven against Pattison and student Munro, whilst Russel and Maclean were found Not Guilty. Following the case, Pattison was in disgrace in Scotland, so emigrated to America where he had a glittering career as a Professor of Anatomy. He died in New York in 1851, and was brought back to be buried in Glasgow Necropolis in 1852.

Later doubt has been cast on the jaw being Mrs McAllister at all. It, along with other body parts, were given a second funeral and interred in her tomb, but it may be the case that the original body was whisked away elsewhere. Geoff Holder points to a theory put forward by Ted Ramsey in his book *Don't Walk Down College Street,* that Pattison was set up. There was a racket in Glasgow whereby gravediggers and undertakers made a profitable sideline in selling fresh bodies to anatomists before funerals took place. Pattison, Ramsey argues, turned down this 'service', instead getting his students to dig up

57

corpses, which was altogether cheaper. So the tomb of high standing citizen, Mrs McAllister was broken into, with clues deliberately left implicating Granville Sharp Pattison. Whether or not this is the truth, it is unclear.

Over a decade later, the murder trial of serial killers Burke and Hare played a role in raising awareness of the difficulties involved in finding bodies for dissection, not to mention horrifying the general public. The unpalatable pair cottoned on to how much money was to be made selling bodies to Anatomists in Edinburgh after taking in the fresh body of a tenant who had died in Hare's lodging house. They preferred murder to digging up bodies, and in 1828, killed several people, whose bodies were sold on to the assistants of Dr Robert Knox at Edinburgh University. This helped pave the way to the 1832 Anatomy Act, which allowed the unclaimed bodies of paupers in Poor Houses and hospitals be used by medical schools for dissection. The schools were also subjected to regulation, and so the gory days of bodysnatching came to a close

A curious incident during the heady days of bodysnatching occurred at Anderson's Institute in November 1818, but had nothing to do with the Resurrectionists. Anderson's Institute was established in 1796 after provision was made in the will of John Anderson, Professor of Natural Philosophy at Glasgow University. Originally, faculties of Law, Medicine, Arts and Theology were to be established, though Law and Theology didn't see the light of day. Classes were given in science, maths, music and art, as well as classes for Glasgow's mechanics. The Medical School was an important part of Anderson's, becoming a separate entity after the Institute merged with other educational establishments in 1887 to form Glasgow and West of Scotland Technical College. In 1947.The

Medical School merged with the Glasgow University Medical Faculty, whilst in 1964, the Technical College became the University of Strathclyde with the granting of a Royal Charter.

But to return to the 4th of November 1818, Glasgow University's Professor of Anatomy carried out an experiment with a senior lecturer of the Andersonian, Dr Andrew Ure that has been wrongly credited by some as part of the inspiration for Mary Shelley's *Frankenstein* – this is despite the fact that Shelley's novel was actually published eight months previously. The experiment in question was the galvanism of Matthew Clydesdale, an executed murderer. Clydesdale had been found guilty of murdering eighty year old Alexander Love near Airdrie. For some reason, Clydesdale, who is described in a contemporary report of his trial as a collier, had a longstanding grudge with Love. The two met by chance at a coal pit in Lanark, when Clydesdale beat Love to death with a pick axe. The evidence given by Love's son was convincing, resulting in Clydesdale being sentenced to hanging and dissection.

The day of execution was November 10, when Clydesdale and Simon Ross, sentenced to death for theft, were hung in Jail Square before a large crowd at 2.45 pm. The bodies were left hanging for the mandatory hour, before Clydesdale's corpse was taken by cart to the Andersonian's Anatomy theatre, where Dr Ure and Professor Jeffray were waiting. A fair part of the crowd followed. Ure had set up a galvanic battery and the London's Morning Post of the 10th of November gives the following account:

"A number of experiments in galvanism were forthwith made. The convulsions excited were so strong, that the limbs were thrown in every direction. The scene had such an effect that a

person present fainted. Incisions were made in various parts of the body for the purpose of applying the galvanic power."

Curiously, not many of the Glasgow papers reported on the experiment. Dr Andrew Ure later wrote a memoir of the experiment and also gave a lecture on it. It seemingly disappeared into obscurity until the 1860s when Peter Mackenzie, author of *Reminiscences of Old Glasgow*, gave a particularly juicy version of events that has been accepted by some as a true factual account. Mackenzie also claimed to have been present. He claimed that Dr Ure and Professor Jeffray were attempting to bring Clydesdale back to life. Chaos ensued, with Professor Jeffray then taking matters into his own hands by sending the supposedly reanimated corpse back to the other side by stabbing it in the throat with a scalpel. Thus a totally exaggerated legend was born. This was one of the last times an executed criminal was sent for dissection in Scotland.

Bibliography

Ghosts in the Railways

Books

Halliday, Ron (2008) *Haunted Glasgow*, Ayr: Fort Press

Herbert, W.B (1989) *Railway Ghosts and Phantom,* Newton Abbot: Redwood Press

Terry, Chris (2008) *Second City: Glasgow Photographs 1860 - 1960,* Ayr: Fort Press

Underwood, Peter (2013) *Where The Ghosts Walk*, London: Souvenir Press

Websites

"Industry and Technology: Vehicles and Locomotives" by John R Hume, The Glasgow Story
http://www.theglasgowstory.com/story/?id=TGSDE09

"St Enoch Square" by Chris Jones, Glasgow History
http://www.glasgowhistory.com/category/st-enoch-square

"Glasgow Central Station" Wikipedia
https://en.wikipedia.org/wiki/Glasgow_Central_station

"A Ride on the Clockwork Orange – Legends of the Glasgow Subway" by M J Steel Collins, Ghostly Aspects https://ghostlyaspectsfolklore.wordpress.com/2012/10/26/a-ride-on-the-clockwork-orange-legends-of-the-glasgow-subway-by-m-j-steel/

"Scotland's Landscapes" BBC
http://www.bbc.co.uk/scotland/landscapes/springburn/

"Glasgow Subway" SPT Corporate Information
http://www.spt.co.uk/corporate/about/our-services/glasgow-subway/

Hidden Glasgow Forums
http://www.hiddenglasgow.com/forums/viewtopic.php?f=3&t=495&p=5385&hilit=ghosts#p5385

"Station Secrets: Behind The Scenes At Glasgow Central"
BBC News 7 November 2014

http://www.hiddenglasgow.com/forums/viewtopic.php?f=3&t=495&p=5385&hilit=ghosts#p5385

The Ghost Club Central Station Investigation 2013
http://www.ghostclub.org.uk/investigations/Central%20Station%20Glasgow%202013.pdf

"Haunted..ooh yes!" Trip Adviser Review 18 November 2012
https://www.tripadvisor.co.uk/ShowUserReviews-g186534-d1874829-r145686427-Grand_Central_Hotel-Glasgow_Scotland.html

"A Lavish Make Over For Glasgow's Grand Central Hotel"
Metro 24 February 2011

http://metro.co.uk/2011/02/24/glasgows-grand-central-hotel-has-lavish-makeover-640848/

Glasgow Grand Central Hotel website
https://www.grandcentralhotel.co.uk/partner/glasgow-grand-central-hotel/

The Witches of Paisley and Pollok

Books

Holder, Geoff (2011), *Paranormal Glasgow*, Stroud: The History Press

Holder, Geoff (2013) *Poltergeist Over Scotland,* Stroud: The History Press

Kingshall, Sophia; Westwood, Jennifer (eds) (2011) *The Lore of Scotlandi: A Guide to Scottish Legends*, London: Random House

McLachlan, Hugh, V (2006), *The Kirk, Satan and Salem: A History of the Witches of Renfrewshire*, Edinburgh: The Grimsay Press

Miller, Joyce (2004), *Magic and Witchcraft in Scotland,* Prestonpans: Goblinshead

Seafield, Lily (2002) *Scottish Witches and Wizards,* Broxburn: Lomond Books

Websites

"Witchcraft on the High Seas: King James and the North Berwick Witch Trials" Carolyn Emerick 18 August 2016 (Updated) http://carolynemerick.hubpages.com/hub/Witchcraft-on-the-High-Seas-The-Voyage-of-King-James-that-resulted-in-the-North-Berwick-Witch-Trials

Survey of Scottish Witchcraft Julian Goodare, Lauren Martin, Joyce Miller and Louise Yeoman, 'The Survey of Scottish Witchcraft', http://www.shca.ed.ac.uk/witches/ (archived January 2003)

"History of Inverkip Church" Inverkip Church http://www.inverkip.org.uk/inverkip-church-a-brief-history.html

"The Witches 1697" Paisley.Org http://www.paisley.org.uk/paisley-history/witches/

"The 'powerful myth' of the Paisley Curse" BBC News 8 June 2012 http://www.bbc.co.uk/news/uk-scotland-glasgow-west-18366305

A Clydebuilt Haunt in America

Books

Clune, Brian; Davis, Bob (2014) *Haunted America: The Ghosts of the Queen Mary,* Stroud: The History Press

McCutcheon, Jeannette (2000) *RMS Queen Mary: Transatlantic Masterpiece,* Stroud: Tempus

Wlordarski, Robert James; Wlodarski, Anne Powell (1995/2000) *The Haunted Queen Mary, Long Beach California,* California: G-Host Publishing

Websites

"Dining With The Spirits" Queen Mary Website
http://www.queenmary.com/tours-exhibits/attractions-night/dining-with-the-spirits/

Documentaries

"Most Haunted" Queen Mary parts 1 and 2, 2005

The Poltergeist's Knock

Books

Halliday, Ron (2008) *Haunted Glasgow,* Ayr: Fort Press

Holder, Geoff (2013) *Poltergeist Over Scotland,* Stroud: The History Press

Holder, Geoff (2012) *What Is A Poltergeist,* FW Media

Underwood, Peter (1975) *A Gazetteer of Scottish Ghosts,* London: Fontana

Websites

"A Trip Through Paranormal Newsprint" Ghostly Aspects 1 May 2013
https://ghostlyaspectsfolklore.wordpress.com/2013/05/01/a-trip-through-paranormal-newsprint-by-m-j-steel-collins/

"Archie Roy Obituary" 9 July 2013 Tom Ruffles
http://tomruffles.blogspot.co.uk/2013/07/archie-roy-obituary.html

"The Glenburn Paisley Poltergiest" 14 January 2015 Sinister Cookies blog (no longer available)

Newpapers

"Noises in the night – and the suspect is a spirit" The Glasgow Herald 17 January 1975
https://news.google.com/newspapers?id=Zo9AAAAAIBAJ&sjid=4KQMAAAAIBAJ&pg=6049%2C2907928

Ghosts, Galvanisation and Grave Robbers in the Ivory Towers

Books

Brown, AL; Moss, Michael (1996) *The University of Glasgow: 1451 – 1996,* Edinburgh: University of Edinburgh Press

Holder, Geoff (2008) *The Guide To Mysterious Glasgow*, Stroud: The History Press

Holder, Geoff (2010) *Scottish Bodysnatchers: A Gazetteer,* Stroud: The History Press

Websites

"The Papal Bull" University of Glasgow Website
http://www.universitystory.gla.ac.uk/papal-bull/

"University, Glasgow 1451 – 1870" Glasgow History
http://www.glasgowhistory.co.uk/Books/EastGlasgowDictiona
ry/EastGlasgowArticles/University.htm

"The University of Glasgow" Wikipedia
http://en.wikipedia.org/wiki/University_of_Glasgow

"Change" University of Glasgow website (no longer available)

"Pearce Lodge" The University of Glasgow Story
http://www.universitystory.gla.ac.uk/building/?id=10

"University of Glasgow Old and New" Special Collections, University of Glasgow Library
http://special.lib.gla.ac.uk/exhibns/month/july2008.html

"The Galvanisation of Matthew Clydesdale" by David A Stevenson, Science on the Streets
http://scienceonstreets.phys.strath.ac.uk/new/Galvanisation.html

"On This Day: 4 November" The University of Glasgow Story
http://www.universitystory.gla.ac.uk/on-this-day/?day=4&month=11

Newpapers

Report on the trial of Grant Pattison et al, 9 June 1814, Caledonian Mercury

Report on the trial of Mathew Clydesdale, 14 October 1818, Morning Post, London

Report on the execution of Mathew Clydesdale, 10 November 1818, Morning Post, London

Unpublished Manuscripts

"The Ghost Is Just The Sign" Mandy Collins Undergraduate Dissertation, 2009, Dept of Sociology, University Of Glasgow

Other

The Scottish Society of the History of Medicine, founded April, 1948, Report of Proceedings, Session 2006 – 2007 and Session 2007 – 2008 - THE SOURCES OF CADAVERS FOR THE GLASGOW MEDICAL SCHOOLS IN THE EARLY 19TH CENTURY (Stuart MacDonald)

Printed in Great Britain
by Amazon